PC PASCHAL CREATION PUBLICATION

10x Your Sales Productivity
The Ultimate Salesforce Automation Guide

First published by PC PASCHAL CREATION PUBLICATION 2024

Copyright © 2024 by PC PASCHAL CREATION PUBLICATION

All rights reserved. No part of this publication may be reproduced, stored or transmitted in any form or by any means, electronic, mechanical, photocopying, recording, scanning, or otherwise without written permission from the publisher. It is illegal to copy this book, post it to a website, or distribute it by any other means without permission.

First edition

This book was professionally typeset on Reedsy.
Find out more at reedsy.com

Contents

I   10x Your Sales Productivity: The Ultimate Salesforce Automation Guide

Welcome to Salesforce Automation	3
Overview of Salesforce Automation	3
Importance for Sales and Marketing Productivity	4
Goals and Structure of the Book	6
Salesforce Automation Fundamentals	8
Understanding Salesforce Automation	8
Definition and Key Concepts	8
Benefits for Sales and Marketing Teams	9
Salesforce Architecture Overview	11
Multi-Tenant and Metadata-Driven Framework	11
Core Components and Technology Stack	13
Solution Architecture for Sales Productivity	16
Designing Scalable Solutions	16
Solution Architecture Principles	16
Custom vs. Out-of-the-Box Solutions	18
Creating an End-to-End Solution Blueprint	20
Essential Artifacts and Documentation	20
Case Studies and Examples	22
Data Architecture and Management	24
Data Modeling in Salesforce	24
Key Considerations and Best Practices	24

Designing for Large Data Volumes	26
Data Migration and Archiving	27
Strategies and Tools for Efficient Data Handling	28
Data Quality and Integrity	29
Security Architecture and Compliance	31
Securing Salesforce Data	31
Security Best Practices and Considerations	31
Sharing and Visibility Controls	33
Compliance and Governance	35
Meeting Industry Standards and Regulations	35
Integration Architecture for Sales and Marketing	38
Integration Patterns and Solutions	38
Connecting Salesforce with Other Systems	38
Integration Tools and Best Practices	40
Use Cases and Implementation Strategies	42
Real-World Examples of Successful Integrations	42
Implementation Strategies	43
Identity and Access Management	46
Managing User Identities and Access	46
Key Considerations and Life cycle Stages	46
Implementing Access Control Policies	48
Enhancing Security with Identity Management	49
Techniques for Secure Authentication and Authorization	49
Monitoring and Response	51
Mobile Solutions and Salesforce	53
Designing Mobile Applications	53
Salesforce Mobile Architecture and Options	53
Best Practices for Mobile Solution Design	55
Boosting Sales Productivity with Mobile Tools	57
Examples and Success Stories	57
Implementation Strategies	59

- DevOps and Development Lifecycle — 61
  - Principles of DevOps in Salesforce — 61
    - Implementing Continuous Integration and Deployment — 61
    - Best Practices for Development and Operations — 64
  - Lifecycle Management Strategies — 65
    - Ensuring Successful Implementation and Ongoing Improvements — 65
    - Case Studies and Examples — 67
- Leveraging Salesforce for Sales and Marketing Automation — 69
  - Automating Sales Processes — 69
    - Tools and Techniques for Sales Automation — 69
    - Improving Lead Management and Conversion Rates — 71
  - Marketing Automation with Salesforce — 73
    - Campaign Management and Tracking — 73
    - Personalization and Customer Engagement — 75
    - Case Studies and Examples — 77
- Advanced Strategies and Future Trends — 79
  - Emerging Trends in Salesforce Automation — 79
    - AI and Machine Learning Integration — 79
    - Predictive Analytics and Data-Driven Decision Making — 81
  - Future-Proofing Your Salesforce Strategy — 82
    - Adapting to Changes and Evolving Technologies — 82
    - Continuous Learning and Development — 83
    - Case Studies and Examples — 84
- Conclusion — 86
  - Recap and Key Takeaways — 86
    - Summary of Main Points and Strategies — 86
  - Next Steps for Implementation — 89
    - Actionable Steps to Apply the Concepts — 89
    - Resources for Further Learning — 90
- Appendices — 93

Glossary of Terms	93
Resources and Tools	95
Templates and Checklists	97

I

10x Your Sales Productivity: The Ultimate Salesforce Automation Guide

Dear Reader, Thank you for taking the time to read "10x Your Sales Productivity: The Ultimate Salesforce Automation Guide. " We hope you found the insights and strategies within these pages both valuable and inspiring.
Your reviews help us understand what we did well and where we can improve, ensuring that our future publications continue to deliver the highest level of value.

CONTACT: pcpaschalcreationpublication@gmail.com

Welcome to Salesforce Automation

Overview of Salesforce Automation

Salesforce automation refers to the use of Salesforce's suite of tools and features to streamline and enhance sales processes, marketing activities, and overall business operations. At its core, Salesforce automation leverages the robust capabilities of the Salesforce platform to automate routine tasks, manage complex workflows, and provide valuable insights that drive efficiency and productivity.

Salesforce, as a leading Customer Relationship Management (CRM) platform, offers a wide range of automation features that help organizations manage their sales and marketing efforts more effectively. Automation in Salesforce involves several key components:

1. **Lead Management**: Automating lead capture, qualification, and assignment to ensure timely follow-ups and increased conversion rates.

1. **Opportunity Management:** Streamlining the sales process from prospecting to closing deals by automating task assignments, reminders, and notifications.

1. **Marketing Automation:** Automating marketing campaigns, including email marketing, social media posts, and targeted advertising, to engage prospects and customers more effectively.
2. **Reporting and Analytics:** Automating the generation of reports and dashboards to provide real-time insights into sales performance, marketing effectiveness, and overall business metrics.

By automating these processes, Salesforce helps businesses reduce manual effort, minimize errors, and focus on strategic activities that drive growth.

Importance for Sales and Marketing Productivity

Salesforce automation is crucial for enhancing productivity in sales and marketing teams. Here's why it matters:

1. **Efficiency**: Automation reduces the time spent on repetitive tasks such as data entry, follow-ups, and report generation. This frees up valuable time for sales and marketing professionals to focus on more strategic activities, such as building relationships and developing campaigns.

1. **Consistency**: Automated processes ensure consistency in handling leads, opportunities, and customer interactions. This leads to a more uniform experience for customers and reduces the risk of errors or omissions.

1. **Scalability**: As organizations grow, manually managing sales and marketing activities becomes increasingly challenging. Salesforce automation scales effortlessly with business growth, allowing teams to handle larger volumes of data and interactions without sacrificing quality.

1. **Data-Driven Insights**: Automation provides access to real-time data and analytics, enabling teams to make informed decisions based on current performance metrics. This leads to better forecasting, targeted strategies, and improved overall outcomes.

1. **Enhanced Customer Experience**: By automating customer interactions and follow-ups, businesses can provide a more responsive and personalized experience. This leads to higher customer satisfaction and retention rates.

Goals and Structure of the Book

The goal of "**10x Your Sales Productivity: The Ultimate Salesforce Automation Guide**" is to provide a comprehensive roadmap for leveraging Salesforce automation to boost sales and marketing productivity. This book is designed to equip readers with practical knowledge, actionable strategies, and real-world examples to implement Salesforce automation effectively in their organizations.

The structure of the book is organized to guide readers through the essential aspects of Salesforce automation, from foundational concepts to advanced strategies. Each chapter is focused on a specific area of Salesforce automation, providing in-depth insights and practical advice.

1. **Salesforce Automation Fundamentals:** This chapter introduces the core concepts of Salesforce automation, including its benefits and the Salesforce platform's key components.

2. **Solution Architecture for Sales Productivity:** Here, readers will learn how to design scalable and effective Salesforce solutions to enhance sales productivity.

3. **Data Architecture and Management:** This chapter covers advanced data modeling techniques and best practices for managing and migrating data within Salesforce.

4. **Security Architecture and Compliance:** Readers will gain insights into securing Salesforce data and ensuring compliance with industry regulations.

5. **Integration Architecture for Sales and Marketing**: This chapter explores integration patterns and tools for connecting Salesforce with other systems and platforms.

6. **Identity and Access Management:** This section focuses on managing user identities and access controls within Salesforce.

7. **Mobile Solutions and Salesforce:** Readers will learn about designing and optimizing mobile applications for Salesforce to support on-the-go productivity.

8. **DevOps and Development Lifecycle**: This chapter discusses the principles of DevOps in Salesforce and strategies for managing the development and deployment lifecycle.

9. **Leveraging Salesforce for Sales and Marketing Automation:** This section provides practical techniques for automating sales and marketing processes to improve overall performance.

10. **Advanced Strategies and Future Trends**: The final chapter explores emerging trends in Salesforce automation and strategies for future-proofing your Salesforce implementation.

Each chapter is designed to build upon the previous ones, offering a structured approach to mastering Salesforce automation and achieving significant improvements in sales and marketing productivity.

Salesforce Automation Fundamentals

Understanding Salesforce Automation

Definition and Key Concepts

Salesforce automation refers to the integration of Salesforce's tools and functionalities to streamline and optimize sales, marketing, and business processes. It involves leveraging the Salesforce platform to automate repetitive tasks, manage workflows, and enhance productivity. This automation not only simplifies routine activities but also provides actionable insights that help businesses make data-driven decisions.

Key concepts in Salesforce automation include:

1. **Lead Management**: Automating the process of capturing, qualifying, and assigning leads to sales representatives. This ensures timely follow-ups and maximizes lead conversion rates.

1. **Opportunity Management**: Streamlining the management of sales opportunities from initial contact through to deal closure. Automation helps track progress, assign tasks, and generate reminders.

2. **Marketing Automation**: Utilizing Salesforce's tools to automate marketing campaigns, manage customer interactions, and track engagement. This includes automated email campaigns, social media posts, and targeted advertising.

3. **Workflow Automation**: Creating automated workflows to handle routine tasks such as sending notifications, updating records, and assigning tasks based on predefined criteria.

4. **Reporting and Analytics:** Automating the generation of reports and dashboards to provide real-time insights into sales performance, marketing effectiveness, and other key metrics.

Benefits for Sales and Marketing Teams

Salesforce automation offers numerous benefits that significantly enhance the efficiency and effectiveness of sales and marketing teams:

1. **Increased Efficiency**: Automation reduces the time spent on repetitive tasks, such as data entry and follow-ups. This allows team members to focus on high-value activities, such as building relationships and developing strategies.

1. **Enhanced Accuracy**: By minimizing manual data entry and automating processes, the risk of errors is reduced. This leads to more accurate data, better decision-making, and improved customer interactions.

1. **Improved Consistency**: Automation ensures that tasks are completed consistently according to predefined rules and workflows. This results in a more uniform customer experience and helps maintain standards across the organization.

1. **Scalability**: As businesses grow, the volume of sales and marketing activities increases. Salesforce automation scales effortlessly with business growth, enabling teams to handle larger volumes of data and interactions without sacrificing quality.

1. **Data-Driven Insights:** Automated reporting and analytics provide valuable insights into performance metrics, customer behavior, and campaign effectiveness. This enables teams to make

informed decisions and adjust strategies based on real-time data.

1. **Enhanced Customer Experience:** Automation allows for more personalized and timely interactions with customers. Automated follow-ups, targeted marketing campaigns, and efficient lead management contribute to higher customer satisfaction and retention.

Salesforce Architecture Overview

Multi-Tenant and Metadata-Driven Framework

Salesforce operates on a multi-tenant architecture, which means that multiple customers share the same infrastructure and resources while keeping their data separate and secure. This architecture offers several advantages:

1. **Cost Efficiency**: By sharing resources, Salesforce can offer its services at a lower cost compared to single-tenant solutions.

1. **Scalability**: The multi-tenant model allows Salesforce to scale its services efficiently, handling increased demand without requiring significant changes to the infrastructure.

1. **Automatic Updates:** Salesforce can deliver updates and new features to all customers simultaneously, ensuring that everyone benefits from the latest enhancements and security improvements.

1. The metadata-driven framework of Salesforce is another crucial aspect of its architecture. Metadata is data about data—information that defines the structure and behavior of Salesforce applications. The metadata-driven approach offers several benefits:

1. **Customizability**: Users can customize Salesforce applications without altering the underlying code. This includes creating custom objects, fields, and page layouts, and configuring workflows and automation rules.

1. **Flexibility**: Metadata-driven customization allows for easy adjustments and updates to applications as business needs change. Users can modify metadata without affecting the core functionality of Salesforce.

1. **Ease of Maintenance**: Since customizations are handled through metadata rather than code changes, maintaining and upgrading Salesforce applications is more straightforward.

Core Components and Technology Stack

Salesforce's technology stack consists of several core components that work together to provide a comprehensive CRM solution:

1. **Salesforce Platform**: The core of the Salesforce ecosystem, providing the underlying infrastructure and services that support all Salesforce applications. This includes the application server, database, and user interface components.

1. **Sales Cloud**: A suite of tools designed to support sales teams in managing leads, opportunities, and customer relationships. It includes features such as lead management, opportunity tracking, and sales forecasting.

1. **Service Cloud**: Focused on customer service and support, Service Cloud provides tools for managing customer cases, knowledge bases, and service requests. It also includes features for automating service processes and improving customer support.

1. **Marketing Cloud:** A comprehensive marketing automation platform that helps businesses manage and optimize their marketing campaigns. It includes tools for email marketing, social media

management, and customer journey mapping.

1. **AppExchange**: Salesforce's marketplace for third-party applications and integrations. AppExchange offers a wide range of add-ons and extensions that enhance the functionality of Salesforce and integrate with other systems.

1. **Salesforce Lightning**: The modern user interface for Salesforce, designed to improve user experience with a more intuitive and customizable interface. Lightning includes features such as drag-and-drop components, enhanced dashboards, and improved mobile support.

1. **Apex:** Salesforce's proprietary programming language, used for developing custom applications and business logic. Apex allows developers to create custom functionality and automate processes within Salesforce.

1. **Visualforce**: A framework for building custom user interfaces in Salesforce. Visualforce allows developers to create custom pages and components that integrate seamlessly with the Salesforce platform.

By understanding these core components and the underlying architecture, users can better leverage Salesforce automation to streamline their processes and drive productivity. This foundational knowledge sets the stage for more advanced topics and strategies covered in the subsequent chapters of the book.

Solution Architecture for Sales Productivity

Designing Scalable Solutions

Solution Architecture Principles

Designing scalable solutions in Salesforce requires adherence to several key architectural principles that ensure the system can handle increased load and complexity without compromising performance or maintainability. These principles include:

1. **Modularity**: Design solutions in a modular fashion, breaking down the system into distinct, manageable components. This approach allows for easier updates, maintenance, and scalability. Modular design also facilitates reusability and reduces redundancy.

SOLUTION ARCHITECTURE FOR SALES PRODUCTIVITY

1. **Performance Optimization:** Ensure that the solution is optimized for performance. This involves designing efficient data models, optimizing queries, and using Salesforce features such as indexing and caching to improve response times.

1. **Data Integrity**: Maintain data integrity by implementing robust validation rules, data quality controls, and error handling mechanisms. This ensures that the data remains accurate and reliable as the system scales.

1. **Scalability**: Design solutions to handle increasing volumes of data and transactions. Use Salesforce features like asynchronous processing and batch operations to manage large data sets and reduce the impact on system performance.

1. **Security**: Implement security best practices to protect sensitive data and ensure that only authorized users have access to specific data and functionality. This includes setting up role-based access controls, field-level security, and data encryption.

1. **Configurability**: Leverage Salesforce's declarative tools and features to create configurable solutions that can be easily adapted to changing business requirements. This reduces the need for

custom code and makes the solution more flexible.

Custom vs. Out-of-the-Box Solutions

When designing Salesforce solutions, you need to decide between using out-of-the-box (standard) features or creating custom solutions. Both approaches have their advantages and considerations:

Out-of-the-Box Solutions:

Advantages:

1. **Quick Implementation**: Standard features are readily available and require minimal configuration, allowing for faster deployment.

1. **Reliability**: Standard features are thoroughly tested and supported by Salesforce, reducing the risk of issues.

1. **Upgrades**: Out-of-the-box features are updated automatically with Salesforce releases, ensuring that you benefit from the latest enhancements and bug fixes.

Considerations:

1. **Limited Customization**: Standard features may not fully meet unique business requirements or workflows.

1. **Less Flexibility**: You may need to adapt your processes to fit the available features rather than customizing them to match your exact needs.

Custom Solutions:

Advantages:

1. **Tailored Functionality**: Custom solutions can be designed to meet specific business requirements and workflows that are not covered by standard features.
2. **Enhanced Flexibility:** Custom solutions allow for greater control over how the system operates and can be adjusted as business needs evolve.

Considerations:

1. **Longer Development Time**: Custom solutions require more time for design, development, and testing.

1. **Maintenance and Upgrades**: Custom code may require ongoing maintenance and adjustments to remain compatible with Salesforce updates.

The decision between custom and out-of-the-box solutions depends on factors such as the complexity of your requirements, available resources, and the need for flexibility. A balanced approach often involves using standard features where possible and developing custom solutions only for specific needs that cannot be met by out-of-the-box options.

Creating an End-to-End Solution Blueprint

Essential Artifacts and Documentation

Creating an end-to-end solution blueprint involves developing comprehensive documentation and artifacts that outline the design, functionality, and implementation of the Salesforce solution. Key artifacts and documentation include:

1. **Requirements Document**: A detailed document capturing the business requirements, user needs, and functional specifications for the Salesforce solution. This document serves as the foundation for the design and development process.

SOLUTION ARCHITECTURE FOR SALES PRODUCTIVITY

1. **Solution Design Document**: A high-level overview of the solution architecture, including the components, data model, integration points, and customization details. This document provides a roadmap for implementation and guides development efforts.

1. **Data Model Diagram**: A visual representation of the data model, including objects, fields, relationships, and data flow. The data model diagram helps in understanding how data is structured and how it interacts within the system.

1. **Workflow and Process Diagrams**: Diagrams that illustrate the workflows, business processes, and automation rules within the Salesforce solution. These diagrams help in visualizing how different components of the solution work together to achieve business objectives.

1. **Integration Specifications**: Documentation outlining the integration points, data exchange formats, and protocols used to connect Salesforce with external systems. This includes details on APIs, middleware, and data synchronization methods.

1. **User Interface Design:** Mockups or wireframes of custom user

interfaces, including page layouts, forms, and dashboards. This documentation helps in designing an intuitive and user-friendly experience for end-users.

1. **Testing Plan:** A comprehensive plan outlining the testing strategy, test cases, and acceptance criteria. The testing plan ensures that the solution meets the defined requirements and functions as expected.

1. **Deployment Plan:** A detailed plan for deploying the solution to the production environment, including migration steps, data loading procedures, and rollback strategies. The deployment plan ensures a smooth transition from development to production.

Case Studies and Examples

Including case studies and real-world examples in the solution blueprint provides practical insights into how similar solutions have been implemented and the lessons learned from those experiences. Case studies typically include:

1. **Background**: An overview of the organization, its challenges, and the objectives of the Salesforce implementation.

1. **Solution Design:** A description of the solution design, including the architecture, customization, and integration details.

1. **Implementation**: Details on how the solution was implemented, including any challenges faced and how they were addressed.

1. **Results**: An assessment of the outcomes and benefits achieved, such as improvements in sales productivity, operational efficiency, or customer satisfaction.

1. **Lessons Learned**: Key takeaways and recommendations based on the implementation experience, which can provide valuable insights for future projects.

This approach ensures that all aspects of the solution are well-documented and that best practices are followed throughout the design and implementation process.

Data Architecture and Management

Data Modeling in Salesforce

Key Considerations and Best Practices

Data modeling in Salesforce involves designing how data is structured, stored, and related within the Salesforce platform. Effective data modeling is crucial for ensuring data integrity, optimizing performance, and meeting business requirements. Consider these key principles and best practices:

1. **Understand Business Requirements:** Begin with a thorough understanding of the business processes, user needs, and data requirements. Engage with stakeholders to gather detailed requirements and identify key entities and relationships.

1. **Define Objects and Fields**: Salesforce uses objects to represent entities (e.g., Accounts, Contacts, Opportunities) and fields to store data attributes. Define custom objects and fields as needed to capture specific business information, ensuring field types and lengths are appropriate for the data being stored.

1. **Use Relationships Wisely**: Salesforce supports various types of relationships between objects, including lookup relationships, master-detail relationships, and many-to-many relationships. Choose the appropriate relationship type based on how data should be related and the impact on data integrity and reporting.

1. **Normalize Data:** Organize data into separate, related objects rather than storing all data in a single object. For example, separate address information into its own object rather than duplicating it across multiple records to avoid redundancy and ensure data consistency.

1. **Optimize for Performance:** Design the data model with performance in mind. Use indexing and selective filters to improve query performance. Avoid creating overly complex relationships or excessive custom fields that could impact system performance.

1. **Implement Validation Rules:** Enforce data quality and business logic with validation rules. These rules ensure that data entered into Salesforce meets specific criteria, reducing the risk of incorrect or incomplete data.

1. **Consider Data Privacy and Security**: Implement data privacy and security measures, such as field-level security, record-level access controls, and encryption, to protect sensitive data and comply with regulations.

Designing for Large Data Volumes

Handling large data volumes requires special considerations to ensure Salesforce performs optimally and users can access and manage data efficiently. Employ these strategies:

1. **Use Indexed Fields:** Index fields that are frequently used in filters, queries, or search operations. Indexed fields improve the performance of data retrieval operations by speeding up query execution.

1. **Implement Archiving Strategies:** Develop data archiving strategies to manage historical data and prevent the data model from

becoming cluttered. Archive older records that are no longer actively used but need to be retained for historical purposes.

1. **Leverage Data Partitioning**: Segment large data sets into manageable chunks using data partitioning techniques. This can involve using custom objects or field values to categorize data and improve performance.

1. **Optimize Queries and Reports**: Design queries and reports to handle large data sets efficiently. Use selective filters and limit the amount of data retrieved to reduce query processing time. Utilize batch processing for large data operations.

1. **Monitor and Maintain Performance:** Regularly monitor system performance and data volume metrics. Use tools such as Salesforce's Data Loader and performance monitoring dashboards to identify and address performance issues proactively.

Data Migration and Archiving

Strategies and Tools for Efficient Data Handling

Data migration involves transferring data from one system to Salesforce, while data archiving focuses on managing historical data within Salesforce. Effective strategies and tools for data handling include:

1. **Plan and Prepare**: Develop a comprehensive data migration plan that includes data mapping, transformation rules, and validation criteria. Identify the data to be migrated, prepare it for import, and define the migration timeline.

2. **Use Data Migration Tools:** Leverage Salesforce's data migration tools, such as Data Loader, Data Import Wizard, and third-party ETL (Extract, Transform, Load) tools. Data Loader allows for bulk data operations, while Data Import Wizard provides a user-friendly interface for importing data.

3. **Data Mapping and Transformation**: Map data fields from the source system to Salesforce objects and fields. Apply transformation rules to ensure that data is correctly formatted and meets Salesforce requirements, such as converting data types or merging fields.

1. **Test the Migration Process**: Perform test migrations using a subset of data to identify any issues and validate that the data is correctly imported into Salesforce. Address any errors or inconsistencies before proceeding with the full migration.

1. **Monitor and Validate**: After migration, validate the data to ensure accuracy and completeness. Monitor the migration process for any issues and address them promptly. Use Salesforce reports and dashboards to verify that the data is correctly integrated and functional.

Data Quality and Integrity

Maintaining data quality and integrity is essential for ensuring that Salesforce data is accurate, reliable, and useful. Implement these practices:

1. **Data Cleansing**: Regularly clean and update data to remove duplicates, correct errors, and standardize information. Utilize tools such as Data.com or third-party data cleansing solutions to enhance data quality.

1. **Implement Data Validation Rules**: Define and enforce valida-

tion rules to ensure that data entered into Salesforce meets specific criteria. Validation rules help prevent incorrect or incomplete data from being saved.

1. **Establish Data Governance**: Develop and implement data governance policies to define data ownership, stewardship, and management responsibilities. Establish guidelines for data entry, maintenance, and usage to ensure consistency and accuracy.

1. **Use Data Enrichment Services:** Integrate data enrichment services to enhance and validate external data. This can include adding missing information, verifying data accuracy, and updating records with current information.

1. **Monitor Data Integrity**: Implement monitoring and reporting mechanisms to track data quality and integrity. Use dashboards and reports to identify and address data issues proactively.

Addressing these aspects of data modeling, migration, and management ensures that Salesforce implementations are well-structured, scalable, and capable of handling large data volumes efficiently, ultimately supporting improved data management and business insights.

Security Architecture and Compliance

Securing Salesforce Data

Security Best Practices and Considerations

Securing Salesforce data is paramount to protecting sensitive information and ensuring compliance with regulatory requirements. Implementing robust security practices and considerations helps safeguard data from unauthorized access, breaches, and other threats. Key practices include:

1. **User Authentication**: Use strong authentication methods to verify user identities. Implement multi-factor authentication (MFA) to add an additional layer of security beyond just passwords. This helps prevent unauthorized access even if credentials are compromised.

1. **Role-Based Access Control (RBAC):** Define roles and profiles that determine what data users can access and what actions they can perform. Assign users to roles based on their job functions and responsibilities, and apply the principle of least privilege to limit access to only the data necessary for their role.

1. **Field-Level Security**: Control access to individual fields within objects to protect sensitive information. Configure field-level security settings to restrict visibility and editing capabilities based on user profiles.

1. **Record-Level Security:** Implement record-level security to control access to specific records within objects. Use sharing rules, manual sharing, and role hierarchies to define who can view, edit, or delete records.

1. **Encryption**: Use Salesforce's built-in encryption features to protect data both at rest and in transit. Enable platform encryption to secure sensitive data stored in Salesforce, and use HTTPS for secure data transmission between users and the Salesforce platform.

1. **Audit Trails and Monitoring:** Utilize Salesforce's audit trail

features to track changes made to data and configuration settings. Enable field history tracking to monitor changes to specific fields, and use Salesforce Shield's Event Monitoring to gain insights into user activities and potential security incidents.

1. **Regular Security Reviews:** Conduct regular security reviews and assessments to identify and address potential vulnerabilities. Perform periodic security audits, penetration testing, and vulnerability scans to ensure the system remains secure against evolving threats.

Sharing and Visibility Controls

Managing data sharing and visibility is crucial for ensuring that users have appropriate access to data while protecting sensitive information. Key controls include:

1. **Organization-Wide Defaults (OWD):** Set default sharing settings for each object to control the baseline level of record access. Options include Private (only the record owner and users above them in the role hierarchy can access the record), Public Read Only, and Public Read/Write.

1. **Sharing Rules:** Configure sharing rules to extend access to records beyond the default settings. Use criteria-based sharing rules to share records with users based on specific field values, or use ownership-based sharing rules to share records with users based on record ownership.

1. **Manual Sharing**: Allow users to manually share individual records with other users or groups. This feature is useful for providing temporary access to specific records that do not meet the criteria for automatic sharing.

1. **Role Hierarchies**: Use role hierarchies to define access levels based on organizational structure. Users in higher roles can access records owned by users in lower roles, facilitating visibility and collaboration while maintaining security.

1. **Profiles and Permission Sets:** Assign profiles and permission sets to control user access to objects, fields, and features. Profiles define the standard permissions for a group of users, while permission sets provide additional access rights for specific users or roles.

1. **Field-Level Security and Page Layouts**: Control access to spe-

cific fields and page layouts based on user profiles and permission sets. This ensures that sensitive information is only visible to authorized users and that users see only the relevant fields for their role.

Compliance and Governance

Meeting Industry Standards and Regulations

Compliance and governance are critical for ensuring that Salesforce implementations adhere to industry standards and regulatory requirements. Key aspects of compliance and governance include:

1. **Data Protection Regulations**: Ensure compliance with data protection regulations such as the General Data Protection Regulation (GDPR), the California Consumer Privacy Act (CCPA), and other regional data protection laws. Implement features like data encryption, data retention policies, and user consent mechanisms to meet these requirements.

1. **Industry-Specific Standards:** Adhere to industry-specific standards and regulations relevant to your organization. For example, financial institutions must comply with regulations such as the Payment Card Industry Data Security Standard (PCI DSS), while

healthcare organizations must comply with the Health Insurance Portability and Accountability Act (HIPAA).

1. **Data Retention Policies**: Establish and enforce data retention policies to manage how long data is stored and when it should be archived or deleted. Implement automated data lifecycle management processes to ensure compliance with data retention requirements.

1. **Governance Framework:** Develop a governance framework to define policies and procedures for data management, security, and compliance. This framework should include roles and responsibilities, data stewardship practices, and processes for managing data quality and security.

1. **Training and Awareness**: Provide ongoing training and awareness programs for users to ensure they understand security policies, data protection regulations, and best practices for maintaining compliance. Regularly update training materials to reflect changes in regulations and security practices.

1. **Regular Audits and Reviews**: Conduct regular audits and reviews to assess compliance with industry standards and regula-

tions. Perform internal and external audits to evaluate adherence to security policies, data protection regulations, and governance practices.

1. **Incident Response Planning**: Develop and implement an incident response plan to address potential security breaches or compliance issues. The plan should outline procedures for detecting, reporting, and responding to incidents, as well as communication strategies and remediation steps.

Securing Salesforce data and meeting compliance requirements involve implementing robust security practices, managing sharing and visibility controls, and adhering to industry standards and regulations. By addressing these aspects comprehensively, organizations can protect sensitive information, ensure data integrity, and maintain regulatory compliance.

Integration Architecture for Sales and Marketing

Integration Patterns and Solutions

Connecting Salesforce with Other Systems

Integration is a key component of leveraging Salesforce effectively within a broader IT ecosystem. It allows Salesforce to exchange data and interact seamlessly with other systems, enhancing overall functionality and improving business processes. The following integration patterns are commonly used to connect Salesforce with other systems:

1. **Real-Time Integration**: This pattern involves immediate data exchange between Salesforce and other systems. Real-time integrations are ideal for scenarios where timely data updates are critical, such as synchronizing customer information between Salesforce and an external CRM or ERP system. This can be achieved using

Salesforce's REST or SOAP APIs, which provide endpoints for immediate data retrieval and updates.

1. **Batch Integration**: Batch integrations handle data transfer in bulk at scheduled intervals. This approach is useful for scenarios where real-time updates are less critical, such as daily synchronization of large datasets from an external system to Salesforce. Tools like Salesforce Data Loader and third-party ETL (Extract, Transform, Load) tools can facilitate batch processing.

1. **Event-Driven Integration**: Event-driven integrations use messaging systems to trigger data exchanges based on specific events or actions. For instance, an integration might be triggered when a new record is created or updated in Salesforce, prompting updates in other systems. Salesforce's platform events and Change Data Capture (CDC) are key technologies that support event-driven integration.

1. **Point-to-Point Integration:** This pattern involves direct connections between Salesforce and other systems, often using custom code or middleware. While straightforward, point-to-point integrations can become complex and difficult to manage as the number of integrations grows. They are typically used for simpler or one-off integrations where other patterns may be overkill.

1. **Middleware-Based Integration:** Middleware platforms act as intermediaries between Salesforce and other systems, handling data transformation, routing, and orchestration. Solutions like MuleSoft (which is part of the Salesforce ecosystem) or Dell Boomi provide robust capabilities for integrating Salesforce with various applications, offering features like data mapping, API management, and error handling.

Integration Tools and Best Practices

Implementing integration solutions effectively requires the right tools and adherence to best practices:

1. **Salesforce APIs**: Salesforce provides several APIs for integration purposes, including REST API, SOAP API, Bulk API, and Metadata API. Each API serves different needs, from real-time data access (REST API) to bulk data operations (Bulk API). Choose the appropriate API based on the integration requirements and data volume.

1. **Integration Platforms**: Utilize integration platforms like MuleSoft, Dell Boomi, or Jitterbit to simplify the integration process. These platforms offer pre-built connectors, data transformation capabilities, and monitoring tools that streamline integration efforts and reduce development time.

1. **Data Transformation**: Ensure that data transformations are handled effectively to match the format and structure required by Salesforce or the target system. Integration tools often provide mapping and transformation features, but custom logic may be needed for complex scenarios.

1. **Error Handling and Monitoring:** Implement robust error handling and monitoring mechanisms to detect and address integration issues promptly. Use integration tools' monitoring dashboards, logging, and alerting features to track integration performance and troubleshoot problems.

1. **Scalability and Performance:** Design integrations to handle increased data volumes and system load. Optimize performance by using efficient data transfer methods, batching operations where appropriate, and leveraging scalable integration tools and platforms.

1. **Security**: Ensure that integration processes adhere to security best practices. Use secure protocols (such as HTTPS) for data transmission, and authenticate API requests to protect data integrity and confidentiality. Implement role-based access controls and audit trails to monitor integration activities.

Use Cases and Implementation Strategies

Real-World Examples of Successful Integrations

Understanding how Salesforce integrations can be applied in real-world scenarios helps illustrate their value and impact on sales and marketing operations. Here are some examples of successful integrations:

CRM Integration with ERP Systems: A company that uses Salesforce for CRM and an ERP system for financial and inventory management can benefit from integrating these systems to synchronize customer and order data. For instance, when a sales order is created in Salesforce, the integration can automatically generate corresponding records in the ERP system, updating inventory and financial records in real-time. This integration improves data accuracy, reduces manual entry, and enhances operational efficiency.

Marketing Automation Integration: Integrating Salesforce with marketing automation platforms like Marketo or HubSpot enables seamless data exchange between marketing and sales teams. When a lead is captured through a marketing campaign, the integration can automatically create a lead record in Salesforce, enriching it with campaign data and tracking engagement activities. This integration ensures that marketing leads are promptly followed up by sales, improving lead conversion rates and marketing ROI.

Customer Support Integration: Integrating Salesforce with a customer support system (e.g., Zendesk) allows for a unified view of customer interactions. Support tickets and case information from the support system can be synchronized with Salesforce, providing sales and service teams with a comprehensive view of customer issues and resolutions. This integration helps in delivering better customer service, tracking support metrics, and enhancing cross-departmental collaboration.

E-Commerce Integration: An e-commerce platform integrated with Salesforce can automatically sync order and customer data. For example, when a customer places an order on an e-commerce site, the integration can create or update customer and order records in Salesforce, including transaction details and purchase history. This integration facilitates accurate order processing, personalized customer interactions, and targeted marketing efforts based on purchase behavior.

Data Enrichment Integration: Integrating Salesforce with data enrichment services like ZoomInfo or Clearbit can enhance customer and lead profiles with additional information, such as company size, industry, and contact details. This integration allows sales and marketing teams to better segment their audience, tailor outreach efforts, and improve lead scoring and targeting strategies.

Implementation Strategies

Effective implementation of Salesforce integrations involves careful planning and execution:

1. **Define Integration Objectives:** Clearly define the objectives of

the integration, including the specific data and processes to be synchronized. Establish success criteria and metrics to measure the effectiveness of the integration.

1. **Select Integration Tools:** Choose the appropriate integration tools and platforms based on the complexity of the integration, data volume, and required functionalities. Evaluate tools for compatibility, scalability, and support.

1. **Develop and Test:** Develop integration solutions based on the defined requirements and selected tools. Conduct thorough testing to ensure that data is transferred accurately, processes function as expected, and integration performance meets requirements.

1. **Deploy and Monitor:** Deploy the integration in a controlled environment, monitor its performance, and address any issues that arise. Implement monitoring and alerting mechanisms to track integration status and detect problems proactively.

1. **Iterate and Improve**: Continuously evaluate the integration's performance and effectiveness. Gather feedback from users and stakeholders, and make improvements based on their input and evolving business needs.

1. Implementing integration solutions effectively enhances Salesforce's capabilities and improves business processes by connecting it with other systems. Successful integrations streamline data flow, enhance functionality, and support better decision-making in sales and marketing.

Identity and Access Management

Managing User Identities and Access

Key Considerations and Life cycle Stages

Managing user identities and access in Salesforce involves ensuring that users are properly authenticated and authorized to perform their roles effectively while protecting the system from unauthorized access. The process can be broken down into several key considerations and life cycle stages:

User Identity Management: This involves creating, maintaining, and deactivating user accounts. Key tasks include:

- **Profile Management**: Configure user profiles to define the standard permissions and access rights for different user groups. Profiles include settings for object-level access, field-level security, and page layouts.

- **Offboarding**: When users leave the organization or change roles, their access rights need to be modified or revoked. Ensure that user accounts are deactivated promptly to prevent unauthorized access.

Access Control Policies: Implement policies to manage who can access what data and perform which actions. Key components include:

- **Role Hierarchies**: Define a role hierarchy that reflects the organizational structure. This hierarchy allows users in higher roles to access records owned by users in lower roles, facilitating data visibility and management.

- **Sharing Rules**: Use sharing rules to grant additional access to records based on criteria such as record ownership or field values. Sharing rules extend access beyond the default settings and role hierarchy.

- **Permission Sets**: Create and assign permission sets to grant additional permissions to specific users or groups beyond their standard profile. Permission sets are useful for managing temporary access or specific functionalities.

Life cycle Management: Continuously manage the life cycle of user identities to ensure ongoing security and compliance:

- **Regular Audits**: Perform regular audits of user accounts, roles, and permissions to ensure that they align with current job functions and organizational policies. Identify and address any discrepancies or outdated access rights.

- **User Reviews:** Conduct periodic reviews of user access and permissions to verify that they remain appropriate. This helps prevent privilege creep and ensures that access is aligned with the principle of least privilege.

- **Access Reviews**: Implement processes for regular access reviews to confirm that users have the correct level of access and that their permissions are up to date.

Implementing Access Control Policies

Access control policies define how users interact with Salesforce data and functionalities. Effective access control involves:

1. **Data Visibility**: Configure data visibility settings to control how users view and interact with records. Use organization-wide defaults (OWD), sharing rules, and manual sharing to manage record access.

1. **Field-Level Security**: Set field-level security to control visibility and editability of specific fields within objects. This ensures that sensitive data is only accessible to users who need it for their role.

1. **Page Layouts and Record Types:** Customize page layouts and record types to present relevant information to users based on their role and permissions. This helps streamline user interfaces and improve productivity.

1. **Audit Trails and Reporting:** Enable audit trails to track changes to user permissions and access settings. Use reporting tools to generate access reports and monitor changes to user access.

Enhancing Security with Identity Management

Techniques for Secure Authentication and Authorization

Ensuring secure authentication and authorization is crucial for protecting Salesforce and its data from unauthorized access. Several techniques and practices help enhance security:

- **Multi-Factor Authentication (MFA):** Implement MFA to provide an additional layer of security beyond passwords. MFA requires users to provide a second form of verification, such as a code sent to their mobile device or a biometric scan, reducing the risk of unauthorized access from compromised credentials.

- **Single Sign-On (SSO):** Use SSO to allow users to access Salesforce and other applications with a single set of credentials. SSO simplifies the user experience and improves security by reducing password fatigue and the risk of password reuse.

- **OAuth and API Security**: Implement OAuth for secure authentication when integrating Salesforce with external applications and services. OAuth provides a secure method for granting access without exposing user credentials. Additionally, use API security best practices, such as securing endpoints and implementing rate limiting, to protect data and prevent abuse.

- **Identity Verification:** Employ identity verification techniques to confirm user identities before granting access. This can include methods like knowledge-based authentication (KBA) or bio metric verification to enhance security during sensitive transactions.

- **Authorization Policies**: Define and enforce authorization policies to manage user access to resources and functionalities. Use Salesforce's built-in authorization features, such as permission sets, profiles, and sharing rules, to control what users can see and do within the platform.

- **Session Management**: Implement session management practices to control and monitor user sessions. Set session timeouts to automatically log users out after a period of inactivity and use session tracking to detect and respond to unusual activity.

- **Security Training:** Provide security training to users to raise awareness about best practices for protecting their accounts and data. Educate users on recognizing phishing attempts, managing passwords securely, and reporting suspicious activity.

Monitoring and Response

Real-Time Monitoring: Use Salesforce's monitoring tools to track authentication and authorization activities. Monitor login attempts, access patterns, and security events to detect potential threats and respond proactively.

Incident Response: Develop and implement an incident response plan to address security breaches or unauthorized access incidents. Define procedures for detecting, containing, and mitigating security incidents, and communicate response strategies to relevant stakeholders.

Compliance with Standards: Ensure that identity and access management practices comply with industry standards and regulatory requirements. Regularly review and update policies to align with evolving security standards and best practices.

Effective management of user identities and access, combined with robust security measures for authentication and authorization, enhances the overall security posture of Salesforce. Implementing these practices helps protect sensitive data, ensure compliance, and support secure business operations.

Mobile Solutions and Salesforce

Designing Mobile Applications

Salesforce Mobile Architecture and Options

Designing mobile applications for Salesforce involves leveraging its mobile architecture and available tools to create seamless and effective mobile experiences. Understanding Salesforce's mobile architecture and the options available is crucial for optimizing mobile solutions.

Salesforce Mobile Architecture: Salesforce's mobile architecture is built on a robust framework that supports mobile app development and customization. Key components include:

1. **Salesforce Mobile SDK:** The Salesforce Mobile SDK provides tools and libraries to build custom mobile applications that connect with Salesforce. It supports both iOS and Android platforms

and includes features for authentication, offline data access, and integration with Salesforce data.

1. **Salesforce1 Mobile App**: Salesforce1 is the native mobile application provided by Salesforce, designed to give users access to Salesforce data and functionalities on mobile devices. It supports standard Salesforce features and allows customization through mobile-specific layouts, components, and branding.

1. **Lightning Web Components (LWCs):** LWCs are modern web components that can be used to create responsive and dynamic user interfaces. They can be utilized within Salesforce mobile applications to provide a consistent and high-quality user experience across devices.

1. **Visualforce Pages for Mobile**: Visualforce pages can be customized for mobile devices to ensure compatibility and a user-friendly experience. By using responsive design techniques, Visualforce pages can adapt to different screen sizes and orientations.

1. **Mobile App Options:** Salesforce offers various options for mobile app development and customization, including:

1. **Custom Mobile Apps**: Develop custom mobile apps using the Salesforce Mobile SDK to address specific business needs and integrate with Salesforce data. Custom apps provide flexibility to tailor features and functionalities to match organizational requirements.

1. **Mobile-Optimized Visualforce Pages:** Customize Visualforce pages to be mobile-friendly by using responsive design principles. This approach ensures that existing Visualforce pages are accessible and usable on mobile devices.

1. **Salesforce AppExchange Solutions**: Explore mobile solutions available on the Salesforce AppExchange that offer pre-built mobile applications and components. These solutions can be integrated with Salesforce to extend functionality and enhance mobile user experiences.

Best Practices for Mobile Solution Design

Designing effective mobile solutions for Salesforce requires adherence to best practices to ensure usability, performance, and security:

1. **User Experience (UX) Design**: Prioritize UX design to create intuitive and user-friendly mobile interfaces. Consider factors such as screen size, touch interactions, and navigation patterns to optimize the mobile experience. Utilize responsive design techniques to ensure that layouts adapt to various device sizes and orientations.

1. **Performance Optimization:** Optimize mobile app performance to ensure quick load times and smooth interactions. Minimize the use of large data sets, optimize images and media, and leverage caching techniques to improve app responsiveness. Regularly test the app on different devices to identify and address performance issues.

1. **Offline Access**: Implement offline capabilities to ensure that users can access and interact with Salesforce data even when not connected to the internet. Use local storage and data synchronization techniques to manage offline data and synchronize changes when connectivity is restored.

1. **Security Measures**: Ensure that mobile apps adhere to security best practices to protect sensitive data. Implement secure authentication methods, such as multi-factor authentication (MFA), and use encryption for data transmission and storage. Regularly review and update security measures to address emerging threats.

1. **Custom Branding and Layouts**: Customize the mobile app's branding and layouts to align with organizational branding and user preferences. Use Salesforce's customization tools to modify app themes, logos, and colors to provide a consistent brand experience.

1. **Testing and Quality Assurance**: Conduct thorough testing and quality assurance to identify and resolve issues before deployment. Test the app on various devices and operating systems to ensure compatibility and performance. Gather user feedback to make improvements based on real-world usage.

Boosting Sales Productivity with Mobile Tools

Examples and Success Stories

Mobile tools and solutions play a significant role in enhancing sales productivity by providing sales teams with real-time access to Salesforce data and functionalities. Here are some examples and success stories showcasing how mobile tools have boosted sales productivity:

- **Real-Time Sales Data Access**: Sales teams at a global technology company used Salesforce's mobile app to access real-time sales data while on the go. By having immediate access to customer information, sales representatives were able to respond quickly to client inquiries, update opportunities, and close deals more efficiently. The result was a significant increase in sales productivity and reduced sales cycle times.

- **Field Sales Automation**: A field sales organization implemented a custom mobile app developed using the Salesforce Mobile SDK. The app allowed sales representatives to manage their schedules, track customer interactions, and access product information while visiting clients. The mobile solution streamlined field operations, improved data accuracy, and enhanced communication between field and office teams, leading to increased sales effectiveness and customer satisfaction.

- **Enhanced Collaboration**: A pharmaceutical company integrated Salesforce's mobile solutions with collaboration tools to improve communication between sales representatives and managers. The mobile app enabled sales reps to share updates, collaborate on deals, and receive real-time feedback from managers. This integration enhanced teamwork, provided better visibility into sales activities, and contributed to achieving sales targets more effectively.

- **Sales Analytics on the Go**: A retail company utilized Salesforce's mobile analytics features to provide sales managers with access to key performance metrics and dashboards on mobile devices.

The ability to monitor sales performance, track KPIs, and analyze trends while away from the office empowered managers to make data-driven decisions and drive sales growth.

Customer Engagement: A service-oriented business used Salesforce mobile tools to improve customer engagement by enabling sales reps to send personalized communications and follow-up reminders directly from their mobile devices. The mobile solution integrated with Salesforce's email and messaging features, allowing reps to maintain timely and relevant interactions with clients, leading to higher customer retention and satisfaction.

Implementation Strategies

To maximize the benefits of mobile solutions for sales productivity, consider the following implementation strategies:

- **Define Objectives:** Clearly define the goals and objectives of implementing mobile solutions, such as improving sales efficiency, enhancing data accessibility, or increasing customer engagement. Align mobile app features and functionalities with these objectives.

- **Involve Stakeholders**: Engage key stakeholders, including sales teams, managers, and IT professionals, in the design and development process. Gather feedback and input to ensure that the mobile solution addresses their needs and preferences.

- **Monitor Usage and Impact**: Track and analyze the usage of mobile tools to measure their impact on sales productivity. Use analytics and reporting features to assess user engagement, app performance, and the effectiveness of mobile solutions.

- **Continuous Improvement:** Regularly review and update mobile solutions based on user feedback, performance metrics, and evolving business needs. Implement new features, address issues, and make improvements to enhance the overall mobile experience.

Designing effective mobile solutions for Salesforce and leveraging them to boost sales productivity involves understanding Salesforce's mobile architecture, adhering to best practices in mobile design, and implementing strategies to enhance sales performance. By adopting these practices and learning from successful examples, organizations can achieve significant improvements in sales efficiency and effectiveness.

DevOps and Development Lifecycle

Principles of DevOps in Salesforce

Implementing Continuous Integration and Deployment

DevOps principles focus on the seamless integration of development and operations to deliver software more efficiently and reliably. In Salesforce, implementing DevOps involves adopting practices that enhance continuous integration (CI) and continuous deployment (CD).

- **Continuous Integration (CI):** CI involves frequently integrating code changes into a shared repository. For Salesforce, this means integrating and testing code in a consistent and automated manner.

- **Source Control Management**: Use tools like Git or Bitbucket to manage and version control your Salesforce metadata. This allows for tracking changes, collaborating with team members, and rolling back if needed.

- **Automated Builds:** Set up automated build processes to validate code changes. Use Salesforce DX (Developer Experience) to streamline the process of building and deploying Salesforce applications. Salesforce DX supports automated testing, scratch orgs, and other DevOps features.

- **Automated Testing:** Implement automated tests to validate code changes. Use Salesforce's testing framework to run unit tests, integration tests, and end-to-end tests. Automated tests help identify issues early and ensure that new code does not break existing functionality.

- **Integration with CI Tools:** Integrate Salesforce with CI tools like Jenkins, CircleCI, or GitHub Actions. These tools automate the build, test, and deployment processes, ensuring that code changes are tested and integrated regularly.

- **Continuous Deployment (CD):** CD involves automating the deployment of code changes to various environments, including development, staging, and production.

- **Automated Deployments**: Use deployment tools like Salesforce Change Sets, Salesforce CLI (Command Line Interface), or third-party deployment tools to automate the deployment process. Automating deployments reduces the risk of human error and ensures consistency across environments.

- **Versioning and Release Management**: Implement versioning strategies to manage releases and track changes. Use version control to manage different versions of your Salesforce applications and plan releases accordingly.

- **Environment Management**: Manage different environments effectively, including development, testing, staging, and production. Ensure that deployments are carried out in a controlled manner, and use feature flags or versioning to manage different versions of your application in production.

Best Practices for Development and Operations

Implementing DevOps in Salesforce requires following best practices to ensure smooth development and operations:

- **Collaboration and Communication**: Foster collaboration between development and operations teams. Encourage regular communication to align on goals, address issues, and share knowledge. Implement practices like daily stand-ups, sprint reviews, and retrospectives to enhance collaboration.

- **Automation**: Automate repetitive tasks, including testing, deployment, and environment provisioning. Automation reduces manual errors, increases efficiency, and accelerates the development lifecycle.

- **Monitoring and Logging**: Implement monitoring and logging to track the performance and health of Salesforce applications. Use tools like Salesforce Shield, New Relic, or custom logging solutions to monitor application performance, detect issues, and respond to incidents promptly.

- **Security and Compliance**: Ensure that security and compliance are integrated into the DevOps process. Implement security practices like code reviews, vulnerability scanning, and compliance checks. Use Salesforce Shield to enhance data security and compliance.

- **Documentation and Knowledge Sharing**: Maintain comprehensive documentation of your DevOps processes, configurations, and workflows. Share knowledge and best practices with team members to ensure consistency and facilitate onboarding of new team members.

Lifecycle Management Strategies

Ensuring Successful Implementation and Ongoing Improvements

Lifecycle management involves overseeing the entire lifecycle of Salesforce applications, from initial implementation through ongoing maintenance and improvements. Effective lifecycle management ensures successful deployment and continuous enhancement of Salesforce solutions.

- **Planning and Strategy:** Develop a clear plan and strategy for implementing Salesforce solutions. Define goals, requirements, timelines, and resources. Create a roadmap that outlines key milestones, deliverables, and dependencies.

- **Implementation and Deployment**: Execute the implementation plan and deploy Salesforce solutions according to the defined strategy. Ensure that deployments are thoroughly tested and validated before moving to production. Use deployment tools and practices to manage releases and track changes.

- **Monitoring and Support**: After deployment, continuously monitor the performance and health of Salesforce applications. Provide support to users and address any issues that arise. Use monitoring tools and user feedback to identify areas for improvement and resolve problems promptly.

- **Continuous Improvement**: Adopt a continuous improvement mindset to enhance Salesforce applications over time. Collect feedback from users, analyze performance data, and identify opportunities for optimization. Implement changes and updates based on feedback and evolving business needs.

- **Change Management:** Implement change management practices to handle modifications to Salesforce applications. Use change control processes to evaluate, approve, and manage changes. Ensure that changes are communicated effectively and do not disrupt ongoing operations.

- **Training and Adoption:** Provide training and support to users to ensure successful adoption of Salesforce solutions. Offer resources, documentation, and training sessions to help users understand and effectively use the application.

- **Review and Assessment**: Regularly review and assess the effectiveness of Salesforce applications and processes. Conduct post-implementation reviews to evaluate the success of deployments and identify lessons learned. Use assessments to guide future improvements and optimize the development lifecycle.

Case Studies and Examples

Case Study 1: Global Retailer: A global retailer implemented a DevOps strategy to enhance their Salesforce deployment process. By adopting CI/CD practices and automating deployments, they reduced the time required for releases from weeks to days. The retailer also improved collaboration between development and operations teams, leading to faster issue resolution and higher-quality releases.

Case Study 2: Financial Services Company: A financial services company adopted Salesforce DX and CI tools to streamline their development lifecycle. They implemented automated testing and deployment processes, resulting in a more reliable and efficient release process. The company achieved greater consistency in deployments and reduced the risk of errors.

Case Study 3: Healthcare Organization: A healthcare organization focused on continuous improvement and user feedback to enhance their Salesforce applications. They implemented regular updates based on user feedback and performance data, leading to improved user satisfaction and better alignment with evolving business needs.

Effective DevOps and lifecycle management practices are essential for ensuring successful implementation and continuous improvement of Salesforce solutions. By adopting DevOps principles, implementing automation, and focusing on ongoing enhancements, organizations can achieve greater efficiency, reliability, and success in their Salesforce deployments.

Leveraging Salesforce for Sales and Marketing Automation

Automating Sales Processes

Tools and Techniques for Sales Automation

Salesforce provides a robust suite of tools and techniques designed to automate sales processes and enhance efficiency. Effective sales automation helps sales teams streamline their workflows, reduce manual tasks, and focus on high-value activities.

Salesforce Sales Cloud: Salesforce Sales Cloud is a comprehensive platform for managing sales processes, including lead generation, opportunity management, and sales forecasting. Key features include:

- **Lead Management**: Automate lead capture, assignment, and nurturing through lead scoring and routing rules. Use Salesforce's lead management tools to track lead status, history, and interactions.

- **Opportunity Management**: Automate the tracking of opportunities through their lifecycle, from qualification to closing. Use opportunity stages, workflows, and automation rules to manage and advance deals.

- **Sales Process Automation**: Implement automation rules and workflows to streamline repetitive tasks. For example, automate follow-up tasks, send reminders, and trigger alerts based on sales activities and milestones.

Salesforce Einstein: Salesforce Einstein leverages artificial intelligence (AI) to enhance sales automation. Key functionalities include:

- **Einstein Lead Scoring**: Use AI-driven insights to score leads based on their likelihood to convert. Prioritize high-potential leads and allocate resources effectively.
- **Einstein Opportunity Insights**: Gain actionable insights into opportunities, such as likelihood of closing and potential risks. Use these insights to make data-driven decisions and optimize sales strategies.
- **Einstein Activity Capture:** Automatically log sales activities, including emails and meetings, to provide a complete view of interactions and streamline activity tracking.

Salesforce Flow: Salesforce Flow enables the creation of custom automation processes without the need for code. Key capabilities include:

- **Flow Builder**: Design and implement automated workflows using a drag-and-drop interface. Create processes for lead assignment, follow-up tasks, and approvals.
- **Record-Triggered Flows**: Automatically trigger flows based on changes to Salesforce records. For example, initiate a follow-up task when a lead's status changes or send a notification when an opportunity reaches a certain stage.

Salesforce CPQ (Configure, Price, Quote): Salesforce CPQ automates the configuration, pricing, and quoting process. Key features include:

- **Product Configuration**: Automate the configuration of complex products and services. Ensure that quotes reflect accurate product specifications and pricing.
- **Pricing Rules:** Implement pricing rules and discounting policies to automate the calculation of prices and discounts. Ensure that quotes comply with pricing guidelines and margins.
- **Quote Generation**: Automatically generate quotes and proposals based on configured products and pricing. Streamline the quoting process and reduce manual errors.

Improving Lead Management and Conversion Rates

Salesforce offers various tools and techniques to improve lead management and boost conversion rates:

- **Lead Scoring and Grading:** Use lead scoring to evaluate and prioritize leads based on their likelihood to convert. Implement lead grading to assess lead quality based on factors such as company size, industry, and engagement level. Focus efforts on high-scoring leads to increase conversion rates.

- **Lead Nurturing:** Automate lead nurturing processes to engage with leads throughout their buying journey. Use Salesforce's marketing automation tools to send targeted emails, follow-up reminders, and personalized content based on lead behavior and interests.

- **Lead Assignment Rules:** Implement lead assignment rules to automatically assign leads to appropriate sales representatives based on criteria such as geographic location, lead source, or product interest. Ensure that leads are promptly followed up and managed by the right team members.

- **Lead Conversion Process:** Streamline the lead conversion process by automating the creation of opportunities, contacts, and accounts when a lead is qualified. Use Salesforce's automation features to ensure a smooth transition from lead to opportunity and minimize manual data entry.

- **Performance Tracking and Analytics:** Use Salesforce's reporting and analytics tools to track lead management performance. Monitor metrics such as lead conversion rates, lead sources, and sales cycle length. Use these insights to refine lead management strategies and optimize sales processes.

Marketing Automation with Salesforce

Campaign Management and Tracking

Salesforce provides powerful tools for managing and tracking marketing campaigns. Effective campaign management helps organizations reach their target audience, measure campaign effectiveness, and optimize marketing efforts.

Salesforce Marketing Cloud: Salesforce Marketing Cloud is a comprehensive marketing automation platform that offers tools for managing and executing marketing campaigns. Key features include:

- **Email Marketing:** Automate email campaigns, including personalized messages, drip campaigns, and promotional offers. Use Salesforce's email templates, automation workflows, and analytics to create and manage email marketing efforts.

- **Social Media Marketing:** Integrate social media platforms with Salesforce Marketing Cloud to manage and track social media campaigns. Use social listening tools to monitor brand mentions, track engagement, and analyze social media performance.

- **Campaign Management**: Create and manage marketing campaigns across multiple channels, including email, social media, and web. Use campaign management tools to track campaign performance, manage budgets, and measure ROI.

Campaign Tracking and Analytics: Track and analyze the performance of marketing campaigns using Salesforce's reporting and analytics tools. Key metrics include:

- **Campaign Effectiveness**: Measure the success of campaigns based on metrics such as open rates, click-through rates, and conversion rates. Use these insights to assess campaign performance and make data-driven decisions.

- **ROI and Attribution:** Analyze the return on investment (ROI) of marketing campaigns and attribute success to specific channels or activities. Use attribution models to understand the impact of different marketing efforts on lead generation and sales.

- **Marketing Automation Workflows**: Create and automate marketing workflows to streamline campaign execution and management. Use Salesforce's automation tools to set up triggers, actions, and conditions for campaign activities, such as sending follow-up emails or adding leads to nurturing sequences.

Personalization and Customer Engagement

Personalization and customer engagement are critical for effective marketing automation. Salesforce provides tools to enhance personalization and build strong customer relationships:

- **Personalized Content:** Use Salesforce's personalization features to deliver tailored content to individual customers. Leverage customer data, such as preferences, purchase history, and behavior, to create personalized messages, recommendations, and offers.

- **Customer Journey Mapping**: Map out customer journeys to understand and manage the various touchpoints and interactions throughout the customer lifecycle. Use Salesforce Marketing Cloud's journey builder to design and automate personalized customer journeys based on behavior and preferences.

- **Behavioral Targeting**: Use behavioral targeting to engage customers based on their interactions and behavior. Track customer activity, such as website visits, email opens, and social media engagement, to deliver relevant content and offers that resonate with individual interests.

- **Dynamic Content**: Implement dynamic content features to display personalized content in emails, landing pages, and web forms. Use dynamic content blocks to show different messages or offers based on customer segments, preferences, or interactions.

- **Customer Feedback and Surveys**: Use Salesforce's survey tools to collect customer feedback and gauge satisfaction. Implement feedback surveys to gather insights on customer experiences and use this data to improve marketing strategies and customer engagement.

Case Studies and Examples

Case Study 1: E-Commerce Retailer: An e-commerce retailer implemented Salesforce Sales Cloud and Marketing Cloud to automate sales and marketing processes. By leveraging lead scoring, automated nurturing, and personalized email campaigns, they achieved a significant increase in lead conversion rates and customer engagement. The retailer also streamlined their campaign management and tracking, resulting in more efficient marketing operations.

Case Study 2: B2B Technology Company: A B2B technology company used Salesforce's sales automation tools to enhance lead management and opportunity tracking. The company implemented automated workflows for lead assignment and follow-up, leading to improved sales productivity and higher conversion rates. They also utilized Salesforce's analytics tools to track campaign performance and optimize marketing strategies.

Case Study 3: Financial Services Firm: A financial services firm adopted Salesforce Marketing Cloud to manage and execute personalized marketing campaigns. By leveraging customer data and behavioral targeting, the firm delivered highly relevant content and offers, resulting in increased customer engagement and higher ROI on marketing efforts. The firm also used campaign tracking and analytics to measure success and refine their marketing strategies.

Leveraging Salesforce for sales and marketing automation involves utilizing its tools and techniques to streamline sales processes, enhance lead management, and optimize marketing efforts. By adopting best practices and focusing on personalization and customer engagement, organizations can achieve greater efficiency, effectiveness, and success in their sales and marketing initiatives.

Advanced Strategies and Future Trends

Emerging Trends in Salesforce Automation

AI and Machine Learning Integration

The integration of artificial intelligence (AI) and machine learning (ML) into Salesforce is revolutionizing how businesses automate and optimize their sales and marketing efforts. These advanced technologies provide powerful tools to enhance decision-making, improve efficiency, and deliver personalized experiences.

Salesforce Einstein: Salesforce Einstein is the AI layer within the Salesforce platform, offering advanced capabilities to automate and optimize various aspects of sales and marketing. Key features include:

- **Einstein Lead Scoring**: Uses machine learning algorithms to analyze historical data and predict which leads are most likely to convert. This helps sales teams prioritize their efforts and focus on high-potential leads.

- **Einstein Opportunity Insights**: Provides predictive analytics on opportunities, highlighting key factors that might influence the likelihood of closing. This includes insights into deal risks and recommendations for actions to improve the chances of success.

- **Einstein Email Insights**: Analyzes email interactions and engagement to provide recommendations for improving email content and timing. This helps marketing teams optimize their email campaigns for better performance.

AI-Powered Chatbots: AI-powered chatbots enhance customer engagement by providing real-time assistance and automating responses to common queries. Salesforce integrates chatbots into its Service Cloud to offer 24/7 support, handle routine inquiries, and escalate complex issues to human agents when necessary.

Predictive Sales Analytics: Machine learning algorithms analyze sales data to predict future trends, identify potential opportunities, and uncover patterns. This predictive capability allows sales teams to anticipate customer needs, adjust strategies, and allocate resources more effectively.

Personalization at Scale: AI-driven personalization tools use customer data and behavior to deliver highly tailored experiences. Salesforce's AI capabilities enable dynamic content generation, personalized recommendations, and targeted messaging based on individual preferences and interactions.

Predictive Analytics and Data-Driven Decision Making

Predictive analytics leverages historical data and statistical algorithms to forecast future outcomes and guide decision-making. Salesforce integrates predictive analytics to enhance strategic planning, optimize processes, and drive business growth.

Sales Forecasting: Predictive analytics helps organizations forecast sales performance by analyzing historical data, market trends, and customer behavior. Salesforce's forecasting tools provide insights into revenue projections, sales pipeline health, and potential gaps in targets.

Customer Segmentation: Use predictive analytics to segment customers based on their likelihood to engage or convert. By analyzing past behavior and interactions, Salesforce helps marketers create targeted campaigns and personalized experiences for different customer segments.

Churn Prediction: Identify customers at risk of churning by analyzing patterns and behaviors that indicate potential disengagement. Salesforce's predictive models provide actionable insights to address customer concerns, improve retention strategies, and enhance customer satisfaction.

Lead Scoring: Implement predictive lead scoring to prioritize leads based on their likelihood to convert. Salesforce's lead scoring models use historical data and machine learning algorithms to assign scores and help sales teams focus on the most promising opportunities.

Optimizing Marketing Campaigns: Analyze campaign performance and customer responses to optimize marketing strategies. Predictive analytics helps identify the most effective channels, messaging, and timing, allowing marketers to refine their approaches for maximum impact.

Future-Proofing Your Salesforce Strategy

Adapting to Changes and Evolving Technologies

To stay competitive and maximize the value of Salesforce automation, organizations must adapt to changes and evolving technologies. Future-proofing your Salesforce strategy involves embracing new trends, technologies, and methodologies to ensure long-term success.

Staying Current with Updates: Salesforce regularly releases updates and new features. Stay informed about the latest enhancements and best practices to leverage the full potential of the platform. Participate in Salesforce webinars, conferences, and community events to keep up with new developments.

Embracing Emerging Technologies: Integrate emerging technologies, such as AI, IoT (Internet of Things), and blockchain, into your

Salesforce strategy. These technologies offer new opportunities to enhance automation, improve data management, and drive innovation.

Scalability and Flexibility: Design your Salesforce solutions with scalability and flexibility in mind. Ensure that your architecture can accommodate growth and adapt to changing business needs. Utilize Salesforce's modular features and customizable components to build scalable and adaptable solutions.

Integrating with Third-Party Solutions: Leverage Salesforce's extensive ecosystem of third-party applications and integrations. Explore AppExchange for tools that complement your Salesforce implementation and enhance its functionality.

Data Privacy and Security: Stay abreast of evolving data privacy regulations and security standards. Implement robust data protection measures and ensure compliance with regulations such as GDPR (General Data Protection Regulation) and CCPA (California Consumer Privacy Act).

Continuous Learning and Development

Continuous learning and development are crucial for maximizing the benefits of Salesforce automation and staying ahead in a rapidly changing technological landscape.

Training and Certification: Invest in ongoing training and certification programs for your team. Salesforce offers various training resources, including Trailhead, online courses, and certification exams, to enhance skills and knowledge.

Knowledge Sharing: Foster a culture of knowledge sharing within your organization. Encourage team members to share insights, best practices, and lessons learned from their experiences with Salesforce automation.

Innovation and Experimentation: Promote a mindset of innovation and experimentation. Encourage your team to explore new features, test new approaches, and experiment with emerging technologies to drive continuous improvement and stay ahead of the curve.

Engagement with Salesforce Community: Engage with the Salesforce community to gain insights, share experiences, and collaborate with peers. Participate in forums, user groups, and community events to exchange ideas and stay informed about industry trends.

Feedback and Adaptation: Regularly seek feedback from users and stakeholders to assess the effectiveness of your Salesforce implementation. Use feedback to make informed decisions, address challenges, and adapt your strategy to meet evolving needs.

Case Studies and Examples

Case Study 1: E-Commerce Company: An e-commerce company integrated AI and predictive analytics into their Salesforce strategy to enhance customer personalization and optimize marketing campaigns. By leveraging AI-driven insights, they improved conversion rates and achieved higher ROI on their marketing efforts.

Case Study 2: Financial Institution: A financial institution future-proofed their Salesforce strategy by adopting emerging technologies and embracing continuous learning. They implemented AI-powered chatbots, integrated IoT data, and provided ongoing training for their team, resulting in enhanced customer engagement and operational efficiency.

Case Study 3: Healthcare Provider: A healthcare provider leveraged predictive analytics to improve patient care and streamline operations. By analyzing patient data and predicting needs, they optimized appointment scheduling, reduced no-shows, and enhanced overall patient satisfaction.

Adapting to emerging trends and future-proofing your Salesforce strategy are essential for staying competitive and maximizing the value of Salesforce automation. By embracing AI, predictive analytics, and continuous learning, organizations can drive innovation, enhance efficiency, and achieve long-term success in a dynamic business environment.

Conclusion

Recap and Key Takeaways

Summary of Main Points and Strategies

Throughout this book, we've delved into the transformative power of Salesforce automation and its ability to significantly boost sales productivity and marketing effectiveness. Here's a recap of the key points and strategies covered in each chapter:

Introduction: We explored the importance of Salesforce automation in enhancing sales and marketing productivity. The goals and structure of the book were outlined to provide a roadmap for mastering Salesforce automation.

Chapter 1 Salesforce Automation Fundamentals: We defined Salesforce automation and its key concepts, highlighting the benefits for sales and marketing teams. An overview of Salesforce's multi-tenant, metadata-driven architecture and core components provided a

CONCLUSION

foundation for understanding the platform's capabilities.

Chapter 2 Solution Architecture for Sales Productivity: We discussed the principles of designing scalable Salesforce solutions and the considerations for custom vs. out-of-the-box solutions. Creating an end-to-end solution blueprint with essential artifacts and documentation was emphasized, supported by case studies and examples.

Chapter 3 Data Architecture and Management: We covered data modeling best practices and considerations for handling large data volumes. Strategies and tools for efficient data migration and archiving, along with ensuring data quality and integrity, were detailed.

Chapter 4 Security Architecture and Compliance: The importance of securing Salesforce data was highlighted through best practices and considerations. We explored sharing and visibility controls, as well as compliance and governance strategies to meet industry standards and regulations.

Chapter 5 Integration Architecture for Sales and Marketing: We examined integration patterns and solutions for connecting Salesforce with other systems. Real-world examples of successful integrations demonstrated the benefits and implementation strategies.

Chapter 6 Identity and Access Management: Managing user identities and access through key considerations and lifecycle stages was discussed. Techniques for secure authentication and authorization were explored to enhance security.

Chapter 7 Mobile Solutions and Salesforce: The design of mobile applications with Salesforce mobile architecture and options was detailed. Best practices for mobile solution design and examples of boosting sales productivity with mobile tools were provided.

Chapter 8 DevOps and Development Lifecycle: We covered the principles of DevOps in Salesforce, including continuous integration and deployment. Best practices for development and operations were shared, along with lifecycle management strategies for successful implementation and ongoing improvements.

Chapter 9 Leveraging Salesforce for Sales and Marketing Automation: We explored tools and techniques for automating sales processes, improving lead management, and increasing conversion rates. Marketing automation with Salesforce, including campaign management, tracking, personalization, and customer engagement, was discussed through case studies and examples.

Chapter 10 Advanced Strategies and Future Trends: Emerging trends in Salesforce automation, such as AI and machine learning integration, were highlighted. We discussed predictive analytics and data-driven decision-making, as well as strategies for future-proofing your Salesforce implementation through continuous learning and adaptation to evolving technologies.

These chapters collectively provide a comprehensive guide to leveraging Salesforce automation for boosting sales productivity and enhancing marketing effectiveness. Each chapter builds on the previous one, offering actionable insights and best practices to help you achieve success with Salesforce.

CONCLUSION

Next Steps for Implementation

Actionable Steps to Apply the Concepts

Implementing the concepts and strategies discussed in this book requires a systematic and practical approach. Here are the next steps to help you apply these insights to your Salesforce environment:

Conduct a Needs Assessment: Start by assessing your organization's current sales and marketing processes. Identify areas where automation can provide the most significant impact. Engage with key stakeholders to understand their pain points and goals.

Define Objectives and KPIs: Clearly define your objectives for Salesforce automation. Establish key performance indicators (KPIs) to measure success. These could include metrics such as lead conversion rates, sales cycle length, customer engagement, and ROI.

Build a Skilled Team: Assemble a team with the necessary skills and expertise to implement Salesforce automation. This may include Salesforce administrators, developers, data architects, and security specialists. Provide training and certification opportunities to enhance their knowledge.

Develop a Roadmap: Create a detailed roadmap for your Salesforce automation journey. Outline the phases of implementation, key milestones, and timelines. Ensure that the roadmap aligns with your overall business strategy and goals.

Leverage Salesforce Resources: Utilize Salesforce's vast resources, including Trailhead, AppExchange, and community forums. Trailhead offers interactive learning modules and trails to help you master Salesforce concepts. AppExchange provides access to a wide range of third-party applications and integrations.

Implement Incrementally: Start with small, manageable projects to gain quick wins and build momentum. Implement automation in phases, allowing for adjustments and refinements based on feedback and performance metrics. Gradually scale up to more complex and comprehensive automation initiatives.

Monitor and Optimize: Continuously monitor the performance of your Salesforce automation solutions. Use Salesforce's reporting and analytics tools to track KPIs and identify areas for improvement. Regularly review and optimize your processes to ensure they remain aligned with your objectives.

Foster a Culture of Innovation: Encourage a culture of innovation and continuous improvement within your organization. Promote experimentation and the adoption of new technologies. Encourage team members to share insights and best practices.

Resources for Further Learning

To further enhance your understanding and capabilities in Salesforce automation, consider exploring the following resources:

Salesforce Trailhead: Trailhead is Salesforce's free online learning platform. It offers a wide range of modules and trails covering various aspects of Salesforce, from basic concepts to advanced topics. Use Trailhead to gain hands-on experience and earn certifications.

Salesforce Documentation: Salesforce provides extensive documentation covering all aspects of the platform. Access guides, tutorials, and reference materials to deepen your knowledge and find answers to specific questions.

Salesforce Community: Join the Salesforce community to connect with other users, share experiences, and seek advice. Participate in forums, user groups, and events to stay informed about the latest trends and best practices.

Salesforce Certifications: Consider pursuing Salesforce certifications to validate your skills and knowledge. Certifications are available for various roles, including administrators, developers, architects, and marketers. Earning certifications can enhance your career prospects and credibility.

Books and Online Courses: Explore books and online courses that delve deeper into specific topics related to Salesforce automation, AI, and data analytics. These resources can provide additional insights and advanced techniques.

Webinars and Conferences: Attend Salesforce webinars and conferences to learn from industry experts and network with peers. Events like Dreamforce offer valuable opportunities to gain new perspectives and stay updated on the latest developments in the Salesforce ecosystem.

In conclusion, Salesforce automation offers immense potential to boost sales productivity and enhance marketing effectiveness. By understanding and applying the concepts and strategies discussed in this book, you can harness the power of Salesforce to drive innovation, efficiency, and success in your organization. Embrace continuous learning, stay adaptable to evolving technologies, and foster a culture of innovation to maximize the benefits of Salesforce automation.

Appendices

Glossary of Terms

To effectively navigate Salesforce and its automation capabilities, it's crucial to understand the terminology used. Below are definitions of key Salesforce and automation terms:

API (Application Programming Interface): A set of rules and protocols that allows different software applications to communicate with each other.

AppExchange: Salesforce's marketplace for third-party applications and integrations that extend the functionality of the Salesforce platform.

Apex: Salesforce's proprietary programming language that allows developers to execute flow and transaction control statements on Salesforce servers.

Chatter: A Salesforce collaboration tool that allows users to communicate and share information in real time within the platform.

CRM (Customer Relationship Management): A technology for managing a company's relationships and interactions with current and potential customers.

Data Migration: The process of transferring data from one system to another, often involving extraction, transformation, and loading (ETL) of data.

Declarative Development: The process of building applications using point-and-click tools and features without writing code.

Einstein Analytics: Salesforce's AI-powered analytics platform that provides advanced data insights and predictive analytics.

Lightning Experience: The modern, responsive user interface for Salesforce, designed to improve productivity and user experience.

Metadata: Data that describes other data within the Salesforce platform, such as the structure of data, objects, fields, and relationships.

Multi-Tenant Architecture: A software architecture in which a single instance of software serves multiple customers, ensuring data isolation and security.

Process Builder: A point-and-click tool in Salesforce that allows users to automate business processes using if/then logic.

SOQL (Salesforce Object Query Language): A language used to query data stored in Salesforce.

Visualforce: A framework that allows developers to build custom user interfaces in Salesforce using HTML, CSS, and Apex.

Workflow Rules: Automation rules in Salesforce that allow actions to be triggered based on specific criteria or conditions.

Resources and Tools

To enhance your understanding and implementation of Salesforce automation, here are some recommended tools, books, and online resources:

Tools:

- **Salesforce Trailhead**: An interactive learning platform with modules and trails covering various aspects of Salesforce.

- **Data Loader**: A tool for bulk data import and export in Salesforce, useful for data migration and data management tasks.

- **Salesforce CLI (Command-Line Interface)**: A powerful command-line tool for developers to manage Salesforce projects, metadata, and APIs.

- **Workbench**: A web-based tool for interacting with Salesforce APIs, performing SOQL queries, and managing data.

- **Salesforce Optimizer:** A tool that analyzes your Salesforce instance to identify ways to improve performance and productivity.

Books:

- **Salesforce Architect's Handbook: A Comprehensive End-to-End Solutions Guide by Dipanker Jyoti and James A. Hutcherson:** A deep dive into Salesforce architecture and best practices.

- **Salesforce For Dummies by Tom Wong, Liz Kao, and Matt Kaufman:** A beginner-friendly guide to understanding and using Salesforce.

- **Salesforce.com For Dummies by Tom Wong and Liz Kao:** A comprehensive guide for users and administrators to get the most out of Salesforce.

- **Mastering Salesforce DevOps: A Practical Guide to Building Trust While Delivering Innovation by Andrew Davis:** Insights into implementing DevOps practices in Salesforce.

Online Resources:

- **Salesforce Help and Training:** Salesforce's official support portal with documentation, guides, and training resources.

- **Salesforce Developer Blog**: A blog featuring articles, tutorials, and best practices for Salesforce developers.

- **Salesforce Success Community**: A community platform for Salesforce users to connect, share knowledge, and collaborate.

- **Salesforce AppExchange:** Explore a wide range of third-party applications and integrations to extend Salesforce functionality.

Templates and Checklists

To assist with planning and implementation, here are some useful templates and checklists:

- **Project Planning Template:**
- **Project Name:**
- **Project Manager:**
- **Objectives:**

- **Key Stakeholders:**
- **Timeline:**
- **Budget:**
- **Milestones:**
- **Deliverables:**
- **Risks and Mitigation Strategies:**

Data Migration Checklist:

- **Identify Data Sources:** List all data sources and systems involved.
- **Data Mapping**: Map data fields from source to target systems.
- **Data Cleansing**: Ensure data quality and remove duplicates.
- **Data Extraction**: Extract data from source systems.
- **Data Transformation**: Transform data to match the target system's format.
- **Data Loading:** Load data into the target system.
- **Data Validation**: Verify data accuracy and completeness.
- **Backup**: Create backups before and after migration.
- **Documentation**: Document the migration process and any issues encountered.

Security Compliance Checklist:

- **Access Controls**: Ensure appropriate access controls are in place.
- **Data Encryption**: Encrypt sensitive data at rest and in transit.
- **User Authentication**: Implement strong authentication mechanisms.
- **Audit Logs**: Enable and monitor audit logs for security events.
- **Compliance Standards**: Verify compliance with relevant stan-

dards and regulations.
- **Training**: Provide security training for users and administrators.
- **Regular Reviews**: Conduct regular security reviews and assessments.

Salesforce Automation Implementation Checklist:

- **Define Objectives**: Clearly define your automation objectives and KPIs.
- **Assess Current Processes**: Evaluate existing sales and marketing processes.
- **Select Tools:** Choose the appropriate Salesforce tools and features.
- **Develop Solutions**: Design and develop automation solutions.
- **Test Solutions**: Thoroughly test automation workflows and integrations.
- **User Training**: Train users on new automation processes.
- **Launch and Monitor:** Launch automation solutions and monitor performance.
- **Continuous Improvement**: Continuously review and optimize automation solutions.

Dear Reader, Thank you for taking the time to read "**10x Your Sales Productivity: The Ultimate Salesforce Automation Guide.** " We hope you found the insights and strategies within these pages both valuable and inspiring. Your journey towards mastering Salesforce automation is an important one, and we are honored to have been a part of it.

At **PC Paschal Creation Publication**, we strive to provide high-quality content that meets the needs of our readers. Your feedback is crucial in helping us achieve this goal. We would greatly appreciate it if you could take a few moments to share your thoughts and experiences with us.

Your reviews help us understand what we did well and where we can improve, ensuring that our future publications continue to deliver the highest level of value.

How to Leave a Review:

Visit the Product Page:Go to the page where you purchased the book on Amazon.

Log In:Ensure you are logged into your account.

Rate and Review:Select the star rating that best reflects your experience.Write a brief review sharing your thoughts. Consider mentioning what you found most helpful, any sections that particularly resonated with you, and how the book has impacted your sales and marketing strategies.

Submit:Click the submit button to post your review.

What to Include in Your Review:

Practical Applications: How have you applied the concepts and strategies from the book in your own Salesforce implementation?

Favorite Sections: Were there any chapters or sections that stood out to you? What made them particularly useful or insightful?

Suggestions: Do you have any suggestions for additional topics or areas that could be expanded upon in future editions?

CONTACT: pcpaschalcreationpublication@gmail.com

www.ingramcontent.com/pod-product-compliance
Lightning Source LLC
Chambersburg PA
CBHW071835210526
45479CB00001B/145